Brand New Season

Brand New Season

"People ask me what I do in winter when there's no baseball.
I'll tell you what I do. I stare out the window and wait for spring."
(Rogers Hornsby)

Table of Contents

Preface   1

Introduction   3

Ed Charles, The Glider   5

Jackie Robinson Superstar   7

The Second (For Larry Doby)   9

When the Gods Retire (Willie Mays as a Met)   10

Dave Righetti's No-Hitter, July 4, 1983   11

Backyard Ball   14

Batsman Number 3 for West Indies   15

Roy Campanella Baseball Field   17

B.A.T. Boy   18

Falling   19

Forbes Field Afternoon   22

South Philadelphia Roar   24

The Power of Baseball   26

Regarding The Game   28

Isolated Power   30

Instructions to LeRoy Nieman   32

Where You Learned Baseball   34

Fort Greene, Where There Could Be Piety in Motion   36

Diamonds in New Britain   38

Little Leaguer Grows Up   40

Gum Ball Rally   41

Bench Jockey Nanny   43

Choices   45

Strike Zone   46

Three Up, Three Down   48

Mitt..49

Stickball...50

Fastest Runner......................................52

Legend..53

Busted..54

Walk-off Home Run...................................55

Cricket: Rain Stops Play............................56

Dear Brownie..61

A Fan For Life......................................63

Preface

Spring Is

A field of brightening green grass as the winter doldrums slip away,

Stretching muscles being limbered up after months of relaxation,

Loudening pops of the ball in the glove as arms and shoulders loosen,

Sprays of infield dirt as speedy runners slide into crisp white bases,

Ever more solid cracks of the bat as swings grows sweeter,

Fans in the stands reliving memories of ballparks, ballplayers, and ages long gone,

Shouts of vendors peddling peanuts, cracker jacks, and hot dogs,

A time of hope that a championship awaits when spring meanders into fall.

—Edward Dzitko | Southbury, Connecticut | edwardiantimes.net | IG: @edddzitko

Introduction

Poetry builds community. That was the message of Woodbury, Connecticut, poet laureate emerita Sandy Lee Carlson, when she served from 2021 to 2024. It was also one of the reasons we started the Orenaug Mountain Poetry Journal (orenaugmountainpoetry.net) in 2023 and why we started publishing anthologies later that year as Orenaug Mountain Publishing.

Baseball is about community, too. Says Chris Sloan, founder of selectbaseballteam.com: "Beyond the scores and statistics, baseball mirrors our culture, bringing people from diverse backgrounds together. It's a unifying force, a common language that bridges gaps and builds communities. In the huddle or on the bleachers, lifelong friendships are forged, and values like teamwork, perseverance, and sportsmanship are celebrated." We saw that firsthand when Sandy hosted a baseball-themed open mic at which people appeared in person and on video. It was one of the best events of her tenure. People shared family histories and memories of the game, and everyone left the open mic joyful and with smiles.

This collection, Orenaug Mountain Publishing's second baseball poetry volume, demonstrates community in the simple fact that the writers are from around the country, with a handful being from outside the United States. But it also highlights the connections one can make through poetry in this story.

A short time ago, we met a poetry contributor named Michael Garry at one of our live readings. In the course of getting to know Michael a little, we discovered he had written a book, *Game of My Life New York Mets: Memorable Stories of Mets Baseball*, which takes a personal look inside the Mets' greatest moments and most beloved players. While writing the book, Michael met a former player named Ed Charles, who was originally signed by the Boston Braves in 1952. Charles spent eight years in the still-segregated Deep South playing in the Braves farm system. He wrote poetry concerning baseball and racism.

For this collection, Michael reached out to Edwin, Ed Charles's son, to see if he would contribute a piece of his father's to this collection. Thus, that connection of Michael to the

Charles family is where we'll start our second look at America's national pastime and poetry. Michael kicks us off with a poem he wrote about Ed Charles, and Ed Charles's poem about Jackie Robinson, who broke the color barrier 15 years before Charles reached the majors, follows.

From there, poets write about ballparks, growing up with the game, their kids, and players. Some contributions in this anthology are about cricket, softball, and stickball. We didn't want to leave out tributes to any games that included a bat and a ball.

I hope you enjoy reading this collection as much as did while putting it together.

—Edward Dzitko, managing partner, Orenaug Mountain Publishing

Ed Charles, The Glider

Inspired by Jackie,
Who came to his town,
Ed never gave up,
He never backed down.

He spoke of his struggles
In fine poetry.
Few players could speak as
Eloquently as he.

Then Ed got to the majors
With the KC A's
And proved to the world
He could make all the plays.

He manned the hot corner,
Sprayed hits, stole bases.
With more help from Finley,
They could have gone places.

But lucky for Ed,
The Mets traded for him,
And in '69
They started to win.

They called him the Glider
For scooping up blasts.
He made it look easy,
No matter the task.

And in the World Series
The Mets wouldn't settle.
They battled the Birds,
Proving their mettle.

Ed came up in Game Two
In the ninth inning,
Got a hit and then scored;
The run was game-winning.

Back in New York,
The Mets did not stop.
They took the next three
And wound up on top.

After the clincher
Ed ran to the mound,
Jumping with joy,
His smile unbound.

Grace on the field,
Grace on the page,
Ever the Glider,
The poet, the sage.

—Michael Garry | Danbury, Connecticut, USA

Jackie Robinson Superstar

Since I was 12 years old and living under Jim Crow laws in my hometown of Daytona Beach, Florida, [Jackie Robinson] had been my hero and my role model. His success in breaking professional baseball's Whites-only policy, had opened the door for the Willie Mayses, Roberto Clementes, and Ed Charleses to follow. And with that in mind, the inspiration for "Jackie Robinson Superstar" emerged as a tribute to his contributions. He was a great American who, during one of the most notorious times in our country's history, led the charge for social justice for all.

He accepted the challenge and played the game
with a passion that few men possessed.
He stood tall in the face of society's shame
with a talent that God had blessed.

He banged out hits and aroused the fans
with his daring base running skills.
This great player and proud black man
many bigots did threaten to kill.

But he continued to pursue the impossible dream
with an intensity that at times was most startling.
He hissed at obstacles and tormented the opposing teams
to the delight of his vast following.

He was a "spirit aflamed" though pre-ordained
by God and destiny, it seemed,
To shoulder the burdens of a race contained
and lift them to lofty esteem.

He ripped up the sod along the baselines
as he ran in advance of a base.

Upon his feet were your hopes and mine,
for a victory for the black man's case.

He opened up opportunities that never existed
for the likes of you and me.
This man from Georgia courageously assisted
in the dawning of a new era for thee.

Yes, he made his mark for all to see
as he struggled determinately for dignity
And all the world is grateful for the legacy
that he left for all humanity.

Thanks, Jackie, wherever you are;
you will always be our first "super star".
For history shall record and eternally proclaim
your great deeds in their halls of fame.

So, go now and rest for a while,
for again you shall come a "spirit aflamed"
In the bosom of another black child
that God and destiny shall name.

—Ed Charles, Sr. | Kansas City, Missouri, USA | IG: @ed_charles_fan_page

Submitted on behalf of former professional baseball player Ed Charles, Sr., by his son, Ed Charles, Jr.

The Second (For Larry Doby)

It's tough being the second
one to make history, no one cares
what Buzz Aldrin said when his feet
made the second small step for man
and how many can name the one after
Lindberg to fly alone across
the Atlantic? So, I feel for Larry Doby,
the second African American to play
in the Major Leagues, just weeks after
Jackie Robinson was the first. MLB
made Jackie's number a sacred 42
and did nothing at all for Larry's number 14.
But he faced the same hate from the stands,
heard the same taunts from opposing dugouts,
felt the same pain showering alone while
teammates stood outside. Larry Doby,
nine-time All-Star, Hall of Fame inductee,
his name forever shackled with the first
one after Jackie Robinson.

—Edwin Romond | Pennsylvania, USA | edwinRomond.com

When the Gods Retire (Willie Mays as a Met)

When Willie Mays returned to New York as a Met,
More myth and symbol than everyday ballplayer,
Batted balls that fronted the warning-track wall
And stretched across the broad, centerfield lawn,
Soared unshadowed to become doubles and triples.

The golden glove who once captured those long and loud outs
And washed away the mistakes of his pitchers, like baptism,
Nowadays, had trouble keeping up in the outfield,
As the greatest ballplayer God ever fashioned,
Quickly and humbly realized that even he can't play forever.

—Matthew Johnson | Greensboro, North Carolina, USA | www.matthewjohnsonpoetry.com

Dave Righetti's No-Hitter, July 4, 1983

1.
Out of rags,
a whole-cloth conclusion,
a finished quilt of nullity.

How does one hold in consciousness
that which did not happen,
the no-thing,
the undone done,
the withheld,
the held back,
the absent guest,
the lost chance?

How does memory curl
around the punctured thought,
poke like a tongue
where the missing tooth belongs?

Gone, gone, gone,
grasping for the negative space,
the diastolic moment,
straining to recall a kind of death,
the resolute negation;
to freeze in mind
the impotence of action;
to love equally the pause
and not the note,
the breath,

and not the word,
the loss,
and not the gain.

2.
Let us begin again with nothing,
with a child's blocks,
piled in the playroom,
inconsequential as a schoolyard game,
one random October afternoon—
not the last day outdoors
with bat and ball
before winter's abrupt ejection,
but the bardo just before it.

Begin with structure-less structures,
and build block by block,
an architecture of absence,
of that that is not there,
of towers filled with air.

Memory works by forgetting,
the selective letting go of fact
enables the fictive glow of truth;
the fireflies in the mind's dark eye
coalesce as immanence
in the shadow world's relief.

3.
Here it is:
as the party ate and drank above,
the TV in the basement room
unfurled its blank assembly—
twenty-seven outs and not a single in,
the man that watched with us,
long since dead, the beauty
of his rounded head,
and Van Dyke beard crumbled,
so, too, the image of the woman
he married and
ultimately divorced,
frozen in her thirtieth year,
the other guests
drained away like rain water
down the grate,
nothing, nothing, nothing
remains,
but the sublimity of nothing,
the high art of restraint,
the discipline of denial,
the one day,
those few hours
in which nothing worked perfectly.

—Jefferson Singer | West Hartford, Connecticut, USA | jeffersonsingerpoetry.com

Excerpt from In Common Things *copyright ©Jefferson Singer 2024; used with permission of Shanti Arts Publishing*

Backyard Ball

On Gram's piano: a pale Polaroid
Of Joltin' Joe and two of my cousins
In Stamford among Mr. Coffee drip
Coffee makers. The centerfielder's smile,
A candle flame lit in the seventies,
Shares the company of Burt, my uncle
Who fought in Africa during the War,
And Laurence, a submariner who fought
And died off the coast of Japan. Among them,
Find yourself in memory's grassy field;
Photos return you to play childhood's games:
Boys have a catch in the backyard with friends.
Boys become men, become soldiers, play ball,
Defend what they love when they hear the call.

—Sandy Lee Carlson | Southbury, Connecticut, USA | sandycarlson.net | IG: @sandyleecarlson

Batsman Number 3 for West Indies

About one of cricket's greatest players

In '75, I saw Rohan Kanhai mingle with the crowd
at Cheltenham Cricket Festival, a pitch throw
from my flat. I felt myself in the presence of
greatness though I was surprised close up

to measure his five-foot seven stature,
given his buccaneer spirit, his adventurous
batting. My grandad said he was the one to
watch when he kept wicket on our black

and white TV. How we loved his falling hook
when he landed on his back, the ball
whistling, thwacking to the boundary
as he built winning innings in '63.

We loved the way he swung that bat
as if sure of what he could do.
A sense of theater made us gasp,
as with clear consideration he sent

a ball back over the bowler's head,
or fielding in the deep, plucked
the red leather from the sky
as if attacked by invisible force.

Both Gavaskar and Bob Holland
named their sons to follow him.
That day he had done his stint
to give Warwickshire a win,

mingled with the crowds, first
touch of gray above his temples
but still much more to come.
He was relaxed, even among

summer crowds and pundits,
moving with grace, sure-footed—
the improviser general, honoring
us with his dazzling presence.

—Jude Brigley | United Kingdom

Roy Campanella Baseball Field

As I saw the grass on the field, I lamented
how long it was since a ball game had been played there,
but then I saw how the grass where the infield would have been
was yellow amongst the rest of the green, and
it put a smile on my face to think of
what once was.

—Lawrence Miles | White Plains, New York, USA

B.A.T. Boy

A boy at Ebbets Field, beneath the stands
I gave the players my practiced, hang-dog look
And stood with outstretched, supplicating hands,
In hope some passersby would sign my book.
Bigger than life, the boys of summer passed
On that dirt path, behind the wrought-iron fence
And some would stop to give me autographs,
A boy's bright "Thanks!" their only recompense.
They're men of autumn now. While others play
At B.A.T. they reminisce of days gone by.
They're shorter than those giants of yesterday
(Though most of them have got more hair than I).
They signed my ball! Rejuvenating joy.
They're still my heroes—and I'm still a boy.

—Bob McKenty | New Jersey, USA

Editor's note: B.A.T. in this poem refers to the Baseball Assistance Team, which was formed in 1986 by a group of former Major League Baseball players. B.A.T., to confidentially help members of the baseball family who are in need of assistance.

Falling

AT&T Park, south of the Bay Bridge
On a Wednesday afternoon
With my girlfriend's brother,
An unemployed car salesman
In bankruptcy, who had two free tickets
To an afternoon Giants baseball game.
I was the ride to the ballpark,
Listening to cars sales stories.
Bob's story changed
To the car with no luck,
A lemon for any owner.
I adjusted the cruise-control faster.
My mind wandered
Into a premonition I was having,
Driving on the county road, Nees Avenue,
Ten miles west of Firebaugh,
At 2:00 in the afternoon.
While Bob was telling a story
Of a complicated car sale,
Credit, bad credit;
The portent arrived
Like a camera-angle on a TV ballgame
Zoomed to me sitting next to Bob
Among a sell-out crowd
When there was a foul-ball fly.

I put my hands out, palms up,
The ball nestled gently into my grasp.

From the distance of Fresno
To the BART Terminal in Pleasanton/Dublin,
Where we parked the car.
We both sat watching Oakland
Backyards, vacant lots and parking structures,
On the train into darkness.
Our ears popping under the bay.
We disembarked at the Embarcadero Station.
Took a bicycle-taxi on the waterfront
To the stadium. We toured the yacht harbor,
Entered the stadium from the rear.
Employees fell over themselves
To welcome us, invite us in the gate
Behind the center field.
We found our seats near the dugout,
Home team side in the middle.
Tim Lincecum was pitching,
While having an unfavorable day.

I had another thought on the way:
The Giants will lose,
Just like in Candlestick Park,
The last time I saw a game.

With earphones and a pocket radio,
Tuned in to KNBR, 680 AM,
I listened to the narrative of the game
At that moment, as it unfolded.
Lincecum retired from the mound early.
Giants were at bat, Matt Scheirholtz,
The outfielder hit a foul-ball

That caught my eye as it flew
From the end of his black bat.
The hitter and I were frozen
In the moment, only our eyes moved
As we watched the ball climb higher,
Moving further in the blue sky.
The ball turned toward me,
I realized the intuition.
The spinning orb hung, moved left
To its original position, froze in space
Then kept growing larger.
I cupped my hands gently in my lap.
Saw myself on the prayer bench,
Anticipating the white-hot globe landing.
When Big Bob jumped up his full length
Reaching skyward for the ball.
From the premonition's presentiment,
I was anticipating the landing.
When, from the tips of his fingers,
Bob deflected the ball earthward
Toward the concrete, the green seats,
Into the drink-holder
Of a woman sitting in front of us.
It was wedged tightly,
She struggled to get the ball out,
Wave it over her head.

The Giants lost.

—Stephen Barile | New Jersey, USA

Forbes Field Afternoon

In August 1963, I was fifteen and
the world was still an
innocent place.
Bleacher seats in Forbes Field
went for $1.25.
Three of us went that afternoon
to watch the Pirates play an
opponent I've forgotten.
Many of the greats from the '61 team
still took the field in those days.
Celia, Mary Jane, and I were there for
another game on a different sort
of field of dreams—
Mary Jane's cousin in Detroit
was going steady with a boy she met
at a baseball game.
So, we climbed up to
the bleachers in time for
opening pitch, and
then began each inning
with a series of walks,
(no runs) a sultry-esque
up and down,
moving among metal benches
sharing nods and giggles
when one among us confirmed
sighting interesting prey.
By the fifth inning,
we had scored some conversation,

but the boys kept returning
their attention to the game
so we moved on.
By the seventh stretch,
we gave up.
Detroit fans were obviously not as devoted as
Pittsburgh boys.

—Joan Leotta | Fairfax, Virginia, USA | facebook.com/joanleotta

Adapted from Joan's poem, Forbes Field, printed in Hobart Journal, April 2015

South Philadelphia Roar

October.
The crack of the bat and roars of thunderous cheers.
The streets of South Philadelphia,
where film and sporting legends come to life.
A new folk hero has emerged,
with the use of a cell phone video,
Capturing for all the world of social media to audibly witness.
For the "bank" was rocking in excitement last Friday night.
With thousands of fans who proudly wear Philly red.
Our folk hero captured the pride and the love
His fellow citizens have for their fair city.
But he did not stop there,
Turning his camera to witness
a Sunday night miracle.
Let me set you up for this movie-ready scene.
Bottom of the eighth inning,
and Philadelphia was trailing behind San Diego.
The Showman was on deck and hit that magical homer
For a two-run game shattering finale.
Pandemonium erupted
As raucous cheers were heard around the tri-state area,
Fans crying and singing, "Dancing On My Own."
Our famous cameraman proceeded to hit the streets,
Reaching the center of Broad and Market
While William Penn looked proudly down from his pedestal.
Phillies fans are a determined lot.
No greasy poles will stand in their way of jubilation.
So thank you, Mr. Wooder Ice,

For capturing baseball moments
that I could not attend.
Looking forward to your next October metropolis bullpen view.

—MaryAnn Abdo | Pennsylvania, USA | IG: @maryannabdo

The Power of Baseball

Sports
Have the power
To unite
Unlike anything else
Be it
Basketball
Football
Or America's pastime
Sports are powerful
Whether it is root, root, rooting
For the home team
Or being on a team
And coming together
For a common goal
Sports
Like baseball
Bring us together
They also bring back memories
My grandfather
Loved sports
Including baseball
And watched
Passionately
Whether on TV
Or going to Cleveland
To see a game
At Jacob's Field
Now known as Progressive
Or I think

Of the days
He would spend
Down at the local ballpark
Enjoying games
With his friends
And my grandmother
And before that
Coaching youth
In the Amvets Baseball League
Leaving an impact
As former players
Would still come up to him
And call him
Coach Moore
And I cannot help but smile
Remembering the man I admire
Baseball
And sports in general
Have an amazing power
And impact us
In ways
We may not realize

—Davion Moore, Sandusky, Ohio, USA | linkedin.com/in/davion-moore

Regarding The Game

Our kids show up at the park
dragging their patchwork gear.
Some are there for love of the game.
A couple because their old man
wishes he were still playing.
All like to hang with those their own age.
They're somewhere in the middle of the standings.
We like to think they're special
but we'll take mediocrity.
Anything to not be on the last couple of rungs.
Today, they play the team
that's just too damn good.
Last week, the game was against a bunch
so inept, even their parents laughed.
The coach instructs our guys to stretch.
Two of the players take that to mean
flop down on the grass.
The shortstop and third baseman play-wrestle.
The rest gather around
the boy with the fancy smartphone.
They can't stop shouting and laughing.
They all disobey the dozen or so golden rules
of the warm-up exercise,
The other team is bigger, stronger.
When they prepare, they mean it.
A couple of college scouts sit in the wooden stands.
They're not here to scrutinize our team.
In grotesque mask and padding,
their catcher is a monster.

Then their pitcher tosses some practice heat his way
like he's waking up the beast.
"Did you see that?" says a stunned man in the crowd.
The game is mercifully called at the bottom of the fifth.
But childhood continues unabated.

—John Grey | Rhode Island, USA | facebook.com/john.grey.98031

Isolated Power

Isolated Power "measures the raw power of a hitter by taking only extra-base hits, and the type of extra-base hit, into account." (MLB.com)

Just before the middle innings of his life, he was filled
with the vagaries of youthful bravado. He stopped trying
to make contact and took ferocious cuts, desiring raw power.

Longing to be idolized, he dreamed of clearing the bases
as the ball soared over his imagined gated community
and listened for the restaurant crowd to whisper his name.

Believing power was where the money was at, he feared
lacking both. He didn't want to be a hanger-on, the last player
on the roster who is always nervous about being released.

He was unaware that not even the immortals' careers ended
with glory but like ghosts in strange uniforms playing
for second-rate teams who no longer scared the opposition.

The exaggerated launch-angled swing, which twisted his body
like a corkscrew into the batter's box when he missed, caused
the strikeouts to mount, while the home runs were spare. Life

Was no longer fun. He thought of his baseball coach's philosophy
about making contact and what can happen when the ball is in play.
Analytics be damned. Why play if you don't love it?

He recalled former teammates and game changing rallies.
There weren't solo home runs, but an accumulation of singles,
errors, walks, clutch hits. Was this any different

Than holding a door for a stranger; babysitting his sister's kids;
mowing the lawn for an elderly neighbor; or coaching little league:
keeping the bases full so something miraculous may happen.

—Tom Lagasse | Bristol, Connecticut, USA | facebook.com/tomlagasse

Instructions to LeRoy Nieman

Paint me a diamond,
But not the kind
That takes light in, spitting out
The spectrum of the rainbow.

Paint me a diamond,
Dotted with four pristine bases,
That on a brilliant summer day
Glowing bright white on well-raked red clay.

Today, yes, paint me a diamond,
Bright green grass framing the infield,
Telling us that spring has finally returned
And another season we have earned.

You, yes you, paint me a diamond
With ballplayers young and old
Stretching limbs, tightened by winter hibernation,
As they move from training station to training station.

That's right. Paint me a diamond,
Your expressionistic style
Exaggerating what we want to see,
Evoking our emotions as you paint so free.

Paint me a diamond,
Splashes here, smooth strokes there,
Colors blending, expressing what we want to say
As we wait for yet another opening day.

—Edward Dzitko | Southbury, Connecticut, USA | edwardiantimes.net | IG: @eddzitko

Where You Learned Baseball

On your father's knee in front of the TV
From pick-me-up stickball on a city street
From a little league field at the park
From Wiffle Ball on a suburban block
From playing and spectating
From bleachers to stadium seats
From family, coaches, towns, schools, teams
From listening to the chatter and patter
through the seasons that were always too short
You watched and played with all your soul, mind, and sweat
You sat in a soggy dugout while praying the rain
would end enough so you could get up to bat cleanup
The game stole your heart while you were trying to steal second
You can rattle off stats
but you would play again now at the drop of a hat
To put on the uniform
To warm up in the batter's box, the bullpen
To take the field, the mound
To touch the plate and feel it tingle through your cleats
To take a swing
To cut off the runner
To be there in the clutch
To pull out a save
To learn every position
To have what it takes
All it takes is spring training to set the mood
Your muscles tighten as your eyes run around the bases
You can feel the leather of your favorite mitt on your bare hand

You release a breath and a tear
and give a cheer from your beating chest
ever thankful and relieved that you learned the game
Baseball—it always brings you home.

—Kathy Nativo | Central Connecticut, USA

Fort Greene, Where There Could Be Piety in Motion

To Marianne Moore, who had lived there

I lived catty-corner on a second floor,
Facing your lofty hidden frown
With all the street-noises scored,
And their intermittent crashes
Spotlighted as they were drawn apart.
Brooklyn was on its haunches as if its stoop had failed,
Its soft brown stones splintering upwards,
Its thwarted histories, a hundred-mile stare.

You came home with a plodding defeat in you:
Hodges lame and Podres flailing;
Snider's bat a long club foot
And Koufax, a savage missile's circuitry.
A charlatan trombonist had lashed you with his lower lip.
As a doomed franchise bled out its stolen bases.
Failure had begun
With the fundamentals, long fences forget;
Of runs ignobly squandered.
And shrill pop flies that drove serenity's slow bird crazy.
I knew, watching you, the walks that landed in a rookie's suitcase;
The strike zone, some murdered monster's pride—
A scoreboard's chronological staring.
Yet the steps you took were wisely nimble,
Like webbed feet touching landfall's dumb third rail
And sussing out their strut straightaway.

What I'd give for the balance sheet you'd kept
So as to let defeat stutter its apologies—
When the day was drily done for
And not the druid statistic you wanted to throw away.

—Brett Busang | Greenbelt, Maryland, USA | brettbusang.com | IG: @mamc331

Diamonds in New Britain

The opening pitch of Fast Jim Steele
zooms past the batter.
Supersonically one, two, three—
he retires the side.

Our Minor Miller parks
a single. Dealer Simon
slides in with a triple.
The dirt becomes a haze
as the runner scores.
"There's Dave."

My tunnel vision misses the ground
rule double, the runner stomping
on home plate. I am glued to you.

How is work? Where
in Ireland are you from?

I follow you to the concession
stand. Separately, we order
a hot dog, a beer.
Maybe this is our first date
and we will go Dutch.
We don't stop talking
through the bottom of the ninth.
Big Jake whacks some kind of hit.
Taylor flies from third.
Somehow, the game is over—

the Cardinals edge the Sox, 5 to something.
Weeks later, we hike the Metacomet Trail.
Walk hand in hand on East Beach.

Two years later, an engagement on one knee
and a ring for my finger.

—Nancy Manning | New Haven County, Connecticut, USA

Little Leaguer Grows Up

You had a nerve
growing up on us like that
before we were ever used to
the softness of you,
after we were impatient with
the quickness of you,
during the times we begged for mercy from
the unrelenting care of you.

You have a nerve
growing tall and saying your own thoughts
your arms stronger every day, your grip firmer
as we force ours to soften
while we love and encourage and
in our secret places, mourn the changes.

—Mary Armao McCarthy | Albany, New York, USA | IG: @mamc331

Gum Ball Rally

Gregory Gumball, here at Wrigley Field.
It's the bottom of the ninth and fate's sealed.
Nick O'Rette is on the mound chewing gum.
Some guy's here tossing Bazookas, that's dumb.
Wait, Nick's shoulder is acting up again.
I think it's his altoid muscle, that's Zen.
He's in the big league now; I see time out.
Toward the mound, relief pitcher Chic Dent comes out.
A tidal wave seems to have taken the crowd.
Chic's known for his razzle dazzle just bowed.
There's an arctic chill spreading through the seats.
I see a lot of fans sending out tweets.
Some teen is holding up a sign, "Go Dent."
Well, I guess that would make him a Dent teen.
There's some young girls in the stands wearing sweats,
yelling to Chic. I guess they're his chiclets.
I guess the manager wants to try Dent.
Chic's winding up and not too hesitant.
It looks like it's his patented fast ball.
How does he make it look carefree to all?
It looks like, yes, it's strike one for Big Red.
Chic is taking it in his stride, Right Jed.
I think Chic wants to freshen up, but wait.
I think this moment will eclipse the game. Great!
Oh, wait, here's the ball, another strike. Wow!
The way Big Red is gripping that bat now.
You'd think Big Red hit the ball into orbit.
Oh, no! Big Red struck out. He's having a fit.
Game over. Boy, that pitch kept Red on toes.

What mo-mentos, those last balls were for pros.

—Steven Sohigian | Massachusetts, USA

Bench Jockey Nanny

Coach told me since I was new
I had to sit at the far end next to Benchie, team jockey.
You know, the guy who rides the other team,
beats it like a rented mule.

"Our boys love him,
keeps 'em loose and grinning.
Other teams hate him.
He'll drop some loud whupass,
but I need you near when he starts to mumble
about the ump.
He could go nuclear.
If he goes off on the ump's family,
then, we're in trouble
Our pitchers can't buy a strike."

Soon I hear Benchie start in on their hitters,

> *Get the kids off of that swing!*
> *Draw a chalk outline around this guy and call the coroner!*
> *Put a Band-Aid on that cut*
> *Grab some pine, meat*
> *Your hostess will seat you!!*
> *Just put the stick down and nobody gets hurt!*

Then their pitchers,

> *I saw your fastball on a milk carton*
> *Put a coat on that hanger!*

You're supposed to drop and roll when you get burned!
I've seen better curves on your grandma!

Now their fielders,

Cinderella gets to the ball faster than you do
Hey Pinocchio, throw like a real boy!
Bozo called. He wants his mitt back!

Sixth inning and all I've heard is light banter from Benchie.
We're up two and the boys are loose.
Questionable third strike, but nothing from Benchie.
I relax.

Then a low murmur,
    Flip over the plate and read the directions.
Did I just hear something?
    Get a hammer and some nails, the plate is movin' around.
What?
    How about some Windex for that glass eye!
Uh oh.
    When your service dog barks twice, it's a strike!
I tell him to cool it.
Now he's starting to roll
    Kick your dog, Grump, he's lying to you!
"Benchie. Cool it."
    Hey Dumpire, call home, your mom just made bail!

—William Singer Moorhead | Connecticut, USA

Choices

when I see a pitch
in the right part of the zone
I try to drive it—
it really seems quite simple—
but good choices rarely are

—Joe Kleponis | Methuen, Massachusetts, USA

Strike Zone

Camping
feasting on oozy, gooey, sticky s'mores,
becoming spellbound by glowing embers,
hiking to the top of Mt. Whitney,
loons yodeling as the morning mist rose off the lake,
Marcy Dam at night: gazing downwards at reflected stars
twinkling up from sibylline depths
Friends, family, husband, sons.

CRACK!
Life threw me a curve from out of left field.
We dropped the ball on camping
and made a change-up in our lives.
I became a ballpark figure
who sat and watched and watched and sat
and sat and watched and watched and sat.
No more loons, just ducks on a pond.
I was in a no-win situation.
I pitched a fit and called "Time out!" as I
choked up and balked, "What happened to camping!?"

But, I was way out of my league with these boys of summer
I just couldn't catch a break
My pleas were ejected
as I forfeited
every single weekend,
just to root, root, root for the home team.

I called a family meeting to touch base;
maybe bat around a few ideas
about how we might spend our weekends differently.
But, they tell me,
It's important to be on a team, it builds character...
If you skip practice, you have to sit out the next game...
My team needs me...
There is no "I" in team...

But, you know what? There is an "I" in sacrifice.
In fact, there are two "I"s in sacrifice
and this jock supporter is done.
Time for me to walk-off the field and head for home,
because I am on strike.

—Thomasina Levy | Litchfield, Connecticut, USA | thomasinalevy.com | IG: @dulcimersong

Three Up, Three Down

I held my breath with every pitch. Counted strikes,
left hand in my coat pocket, fingers keeping the tally.
My daughter, caught mid-curve, now fully grown with a
young girl of her own. This image is frozen in time:

Desire and grit arranged on her tanned young face.
Now at bat, she launches an impossible yellow sphere
into a future none of us could have imagined. College,
deaths, marriage, a pandemic, new jobs, a baby.

Her husband's heart failure and transplant, Christmas
with a toddler celebrated through video calls.
And now we are here, early spring. This photo pops up
on my screen, a reminder of what possible looks like.

Is she the same person, only more so? Are we? Or less,
but wiser? We follow the arc of the ball into space.

—Carlene M. Gadapee | Littleton, New Hampshire, USA | IG: @carlenegadapee

Mitt

This old leather finds the ball
all on her own, doesn't really
need me. A million long tosses,
sharp grounders, pop-ups
into the short outfield, lazy
flies, and line drives have beaten
memory into her creases.
Some days, she's grouchy,
has me catch with my palm.
For revenge.

—Paul Moorehead | Newfoundland and Labrador, Canada

Stickball

Summers were a never-ending 7th inning.
And games stretched into the next day
when the sun no longer lit the cul-de-sac.
My brother's knuckle ball was an
experiment in flight pattern,
a taunting array of speculation:
              juking and jutting,
       a hovering slow dance
                      inventing new steps
the batter could never learn.

My fastball was a humming blur of rocket science.
And whoever made contact deserved to
commandeer the moon.

The neighborhood kids were filler,
Portuguese soccer-playing
perpetual strikeout victims
always stuck out in right field
because they were more skilled with their feet
than with their hands.

Today it's the bottom of the 9th inning.
Two outs...
And we are dreamers posing as fathers
reminding our own children,

"Point your toe to the target.
Keep your elbow up.
And follow through on the pitch."

Today I remember belting an old tennis ball
over the neighbor's roof
into his backyard,
gliding around makeshift bases
with glorious fists raised,
as if God was pulling our hands.

—Daniel Romo | Long Beach, California, USA | danieljromo.com | IG: @prosepoem

Fastest Runner

I was the fastest runner
        in fourth grade
short and skinny
        and even though
I didn't have the longest legs
        I was quick
I loved softball

We played at recess
        and after school for a little while
those of us
        who didn't have to take the bus
I walked to school

I could hit the ball
        and boogie to first base
usually made a good hit
        sometimes a home run
I loved softball

They never asked me to pitch.

—Isabell VanMerliln | Sonoma, California, USA | isabellvanmerlin.com

Legend

Once I imagined I was a great poet,
A laureate.
I won the Pulitzer prize for lit
And the Nobel for bullshit.

Before that I was a famous actor
And a rock star,
I won an Oscar and a Grammy—
How uncanny.

Before that I was a star athlete.
I hit 100 home runs and
threw 100 touchdowns in the same year—
What a career.

Before that I was a little boy
Wondering what I would be when I grew up.
"Dream Big" mommy would say,
And mommies are always right.

It's so wonderful that all my dreams have come true
and that I became the legend of my mind
so that I can share my dreams with you.

—Samuel Gluck | Woodbury, Connecticut, USA | samuelgluckpoet.com

Busted

Ace pitcher hurls spittle, grabs the bill of his cap and adjusts it for fit, mitt-swipes his lips, double shrugs his shoulders, blinks hard at the catcher, delivers the pitch. But it's a seeing–eye single–another base hit. Now the bench coach steps out on a stomp to the mound. Infielders huddle. The catcher's en-route. No eye contact's given or in-your-face shouts, but the southpaw looks miffed. It's all ball and biz, bro. The fast pitch? You're out.

the house
reshuffles the cards
cold deck

—dl mattila | Virginia, USA

Walk-off Home Run

Bases are loaded
One crack of a baseball bat
The home crowd erupts

—Joseph Adomavicia | Waterbury, Connecticut, USA | IG: @Joe_the_Poet

Cricket: Rain Stops Play

A flipped shilling lands, exposing a crowned queen
Triggers dialogue between captains on village green
Covers protect wicket from early morning mist

Everyone heads for village pavilion for first cup of tea
Whilst bare handed, groundsman scours grassy dew
Parliamentary chairs arranged on verandas front

Visitor's team name given pride of place
Numbers stacked in wooden crates lined up ready for anticipated scoring
Worn weathered wickets touched up with a chalky paint

Eleven individuals kitted as one reconnoiter slippery grassy zeal
Reformation sallies forth two padded champions
Umpires call "Play" as Church bells peal

Three stumpy wooden staves are so bravely guarded
A stomping snarling serious footed bowler
Runs with feet on fire

A slap on ground by batted defender
Warns the ball not to dither
"Please be straight and short of length"

"Out"
The ball did but dither
And took out a precipitous leg stump

None for one
Bowled for an embarrassing duck
Quaint it may be, but birds of a feather must be obeyed

Numbers start to run from their box
One, twos and none that pass into the encircling ropey world
The church rings mid-day a rescuing hiatus

Only the last stragglers await their doom
But a luncheon rescues their disparaging purple collapse
Cucumber sandwiches and fresh pastries salvage each soul

A groundman appears with roller
In slow measure, the middle is flattened
"Was too wet this morning to roll back for pace"

Mingling villagers now chewing a year's bygone graces
Community at the heart of leather swathed wooden speal
Virtually splined in a willowing endeavor

Enabling people to umpire a game to outwit a foe
To anticipate being thrown a googly affair
Relish the spectacle, almost seems like real fun

A round of applause on returning to the jousting field of tête-à-tête
Whites now stained green peddle the promise of restricting more runs
All out and not a century has yet passed

Tables now turned
Silly mid-on bends over awaiting a dental refrain
Only thirty run chase to win and no longer shadows are cast

Obscure scoring and rules blithely allow a humoring smile
Rain has stopped play
A handshake and participation a reward enough for civility in sport

—Kevin Wright | Lancashire, United Kingdom | youtube.com/@KKWpoems

Epilogue

Dear Brownie

I know it's been more than 60 years, and even though you couldn't have known, I stay in touch in my own way. I'm writing from Dempsey Park. You'll be glad to know the old home field is still there, still laid out with third base just out your back door. I was drawn to Dempsey today to remind myself of who I am.

I am remembering what it's like when you're first choice after breakfast is to bike to the park, anoint yourself with sweat and dust on a June morning, and devote a summer to a ritual founded upon the joy of staking your ground—just you and your favorite bat at the center of the universe and knowing even Ted Williams failed more often than not.

And another thing: I need to let you know that I owe you, that I took more than my share. Took more than my share from that duffle bag of bats, adopted by each of us, all of us. Bats standing tall inside that bag, jostling with each other in that fine-grain, solid wood chatter and testing the kid chosen to carry the bag to the end of the bench, chosen to release all that Louisville Slugger power into the diamond dust we scooped up and rubbed into our palms with a little spit for good luck. I took from that other bag as well, that bottomless canvas bag with the broken handle that held inside perfectly round, perfectly wound futures—fast balls, curve balls, foul balls, fair balls—waiting to be touched, called upon, tossed into the action.

Imagine being called upon to root around in that bag and find the one for infield practice—the one least bruised, least scarred, most likely to bounce true. Imagine what it's like to see with your fingers, to wrap your fingers around all that taut horsehide and tight stitching. To find the one we got back from the ump after last game—almost new. Imagine a bag with only good choices and better choices. Imagine what it was like for a scrawny kid to belong to a team with a whole bag of fat pitches tumbling into his boyhood.

These hard-won totems would lay in waiting at your feet, Brownie, while you pitched batting practice, pitched to each boy trying to find his swing, trying to find what you saw in his swing. Imagine a prince, a rookie, in the presence of such endless excellence. No, I didn't take a ball. I didn't take a bat. That's not what I owe. I took something inside my shirt, under my skin. I took the grit you taught us to find on the field. Sandlot grit, diamond grit we carried home in the early innings of our lives—never suspecting we were playing for keeps.

—John Cruze | Ohio, USA

A Fan For Life

It started sometime in the early 2000s. I grew up spoiled with front-row seats on the third-base side when Wright was playing third for the Mets. This was totally lost on me as a child, but my brothers were hooked; they had to be Mets fans for life.

Now, 20 some odd years later, sitting with my family, glued to the TV, yelling at people who cannot hear me, I totally get the rush, the draw, the thrill. Crying and falling to my knees when Alonso hit "that home-run," rushing home to catch the game, and subjecting my girlfriend's family to watch a team they had no interest in. (Once, I even had the absolute privilege to treat my whole family and my best friend to a Mets suite experience thanks to my job.)

Recently, it has been hard to connect with people out in the wild. I have been too scared to say anything, avoiding crossing paths with those whose views might oppose mine. Baseball makes the connection, though, when there is a slight nod when I would pass a fellow Mets fan sporting a hat, people saying "Go Mets!" when seeing my whole family in team gear. Being able to find a connection point where there otherwise isn't one; it truly is such a beautiful experience.

I wish there were more of this.

The day after the Mets lost and were eliminated from the playoffs, I passed a stranger, and I saw that he was wearing a Mets hat.

"They put up a really good fight."

"They really did, very un-Mets of them."

Being a Mets fan is as thrilling as it is disappointing; I wouldn't trade it.

—Sage Higgins | Kingston, New York, USA | sagehiggins.com; IG: @sage_elyse

About Orenaug Mountain Publishing

We believe that poetry has the power to create community, connect us to each other through our experiences, and place us in communion with our world.

We are committed to publishing poetry that is both challenging and accessible, and to giving voice to those who might not have previously had the opportunity to share their work with a wider audience.

Orenaug Mountain Publishing produces themed anthologies throughout the year by poets answering the call and from the work of those poets published in the Orenaug Mountain Poetry Journal, an e-zine that publishes the work of emerging and established poets.

Submissions to our anthologies and our online poetry journal are always free.

Follow us on Instagram: instagram.com/orenaugmountainpub
Follow our Facebook page: facebook.com/OMPJTeam
Join our mailing list: orenaugmountainpublishing.com/about/announcements

Orenaug Mountain is a 78.45-acre town park located in Woodbury, Connecticut. The park is situated on a basalt (trap rock) ridge overlooking the Pomperaug River Valley. The main entrance to Orenaug Park is flanked by two stone columns with stones that have been cultivated from all 50 states. The mountain is named after the Orenaug people who once lived in the area. The tribe's name means "place of the great rocks." The mountain is known for its dramatic rock formations and natural amphitheater.

From Orenaug Mountain Publishing

Community Collaborations
Instances of Seeing, Volume 2 (2024) with Flanders Nature Center (Woodbury, Connecticut)
The Nature of Woodbury (2024) with Woodbury Public Library (Connecticut)
From Art to Art (2023) with Woodbury Public Library (Connecticut)
Instances of Seeing (2023) with Flanders Nature Center (Woodbury, Connecticut)

International Collections
Lost Love (2025)
Personal Freedom (2025)
We Are Here (2024)
Whose Spirits Touch (2024)
Winter Glimmerings (2024)
The Harvest and the Reaping (2023)

Books
Alpacas In Green Pastures (2024) by Caroline Cornelissen
Thanks for the Memories (2024) by Roger Funston

Poetry
Muse (2025) by Samuel Gluck
I Know Myself as Thief (2025) by Jo-An Iannotti, OP
Time with Thay (2025) by Edward Dzitko

www.ingramcontent.com/pod-product-compliance
Lightning Source LLC
LaVergne TN
LVHW061339060426
835511LV00014B/2022